GW01158195

Original title:
Under the Mistletoe's Glow

Author: Jasper Montgomery
ISBN HARDBACK: 978-9916-94-118-8
ISBN PAPERBACK: 978-9916-94-119-5

Sweet Cadence of December Nights

Frosty windows, a perfect sight,
Candles flicker, oh what a light!
Socks and mittens dance in delight,
Gifts wrapped tight, all feels so right.

Laughter echoes, cookies in hand,
Snowflakes falling, joy is unplanned.
Twinkling lights across the land,
Fond memories that we've all planned.

Underneath the Festive Canopy

Boughs of evergreen, stacked so tall,
Ornaments glitter, they're having a ball!
Sipping hot cocoa, we'll never stall,
Dreams of sugarplum dances call.

An elf in the corner, just can't behave,
Gingerbread houses, oh what a wave!
With each little mishap, we laugh and rave,
Joy of the season, sweet memories we crave.

The Warmth of Shared Spirits

Chilly air, but hearts full of cheer,
Rudolph's nose is bright, no need to steer!
Merry we toast with laughter near,
Each silly moment, we hold so dear.

Grandma's fruitcake, a sight of surprise,
All of our faces, just wide-eyed sighs!
With each funny mishap, the spirit flies,
Together we sparkle, in joyous ties.

Stars Aligning in Icy Serenity

Starlit skies are a magical view,
Frosty breath in the night so blue.
Slip on ice, but a giggle ensues,
Wipe on a smile, it's all we can do!

Carols sung off-key, yet so sincere,
Laughter erupts, bringing all very near.
Magic in moments, some sweet, some sheer,
Under the stars, we toast with good cheer.

Love's Invitation at Winter's Door

Snowflakes falling, what a sight,
Lovers slipping, oh what a fright.
Hot cocoa spills, laughter takes flight,
Love's mishaps add to the night.

Socks mismatched, a true fashion crime,
Dancing awkwardly, we're so out of time.
Warm hugs shared, oh what a rhyme,
These funny moments, the reason we climb.

The Wreath of Togetherness

Wreaths on doors, we hang with care,
But who forgot the mistletoe there?
A peck on the cheek, a quick little scare,
Hearts raced faster than we can declare.

Baking cookies, we made a mess,
Flour on faces, can we confess?
Sweet treats made, but oh, what distress,
Laughter erupts, a joyous excess.

Embracing the Chill with Warmth

Scarves tangled up, a sight to behold,
Hot soup splashed, stories retold.
Snowball fights, we feel so bold,
Winter's chill, we start to mold.

Sipping drinks, a cheeky cheer,
Whispers shared, we keep it near.
Chilly fingers, draw you near,
Funny moments melt our fear.

Hearts Entwined in the Silence

Silent nights, but laughter's loud,
Under blankets, we feel so proud.
A snore escapes, we're quite a crowd,
With every giggle, the love avowed.

Fuzzy socks mixed, what a fashion faux,
Guessing rhythms of our festive flow.
In silly dances, our joy does grow,
Together we shine, put on a show.

Embracing the Spirit of Yuletide

Jingle bells ring, let the cheer unfold,
But Aunt Edna's fruitcake? A story retold.
We raise our cups, spill eggnog with glee,
While Uncle Joe dances like he's lost at sea.

Snowflakes swirl, a winter delight,
Bob slipped on ice, oh what a sight!
We giggle and snort, wrapped in a hug,
While Grandma's cat is all snuggled and snug.

Echoes of Love in the Chill

With chilly breath and noses pink,
Two lovers met, oh what a clink!
They leaned in close, but oh what a blunder,
The mistletoe was a candy to wonder.

A kiss they shared, then slipped on the snow,
"Where's my hat?" he shouted, "Oh no, oh no!"
Laughter erupted, bright as the moon,
Love in the air, with a festive tune.

Laughter Amidst the Frost

Icicles hanging, with laughter in air,
Timmy threw snowballs, but oh, not fair!
With cheeks all aglow, he missed his old Dad,
"Watch out!" yelled the puppy, and oh, how we've spat!

With frosty noses and playful fights,
We wrap up warm on cold, starry nights.
The sledding's a blast, yet somehow it seems,
Grandpa's snores echo, like well-told dreams.

The Magic of Unexpected Meetings

In the crowded mall, where chaos reigns,
A lost shoe, a laugh, what a funny gain!
She stumbled right back, tripped on a broom,
With a smile so bright, she lit up the room.

As kids zoomed by with their winter cheer,
A random bump turned two strangers to near.
"Let's grab some cocoa!" was her heartfelt shout,
Joy found in chaos, that's what it's about!

The Language of Stars and Ice

In the winter's chill, we dance and sway,
While penguins juggle in a quirky ballet.
Snowflakes are gossiping high above,
As we slip and fall, but still share love.

The frostbite nips at our silly noses,
While we chuckle 'bout our woolen poses.
With every laugh, the stars twinkle bright,
Our silly antics spark up the night.

Hot cocoa spills on a cozy chair,
As a snowman grins, with a frosty stare.
We toast to love, with marshmallows galore,
While our snowball fights become the uproar.

So grab your mittens, come join the fun,
With twinkling lights, we've only begun.
In this frosty realm, laughter will flow,
As we celebrate warmth amidst the snow.

Glimmers of Love in the Dark

Beneath twinkling lights, we stumble and trip,
With laughter exploding from our silly lip.
A reindeer winks, while we share a grin,
As clumsy romance finds a way to begin.

Our hot cider fizzles, what a funny sight!
We bonk heads laughing, oh, what sheer delight.
Mistletoe hangs like a conspiracy plot,
As we go for a kiss but get tangled in knots.

The carolers sing, but we could not care,
We're lost in our giggles, dancing everywhere.
While snowflakes drift down, we lose track of time,
Creating a rhythm, like a silly rhyme.

So come share a laugh, let the good times flow,
Our holiday spirit only seems to grow.
In this joyful frolic, we'll make our mark,
Creating sweet moments, brightening the dark.

A Celebration of Hearts Awash in Light

With tinsel and glitter, we decorate cheer,
As mischief and madness draw everyone near.
A fruitcake's dancing like it's got a face,
While we jest with delight, oh, what a race!

Our socks are mismatched, a fashion faux pas,
While we talk to a squirrel, who won't leave from afar.
With candy canes jostling in our clumsy hands,
We swirl 'round the room, revealing our plans.

The lights start to twinkle, igniting our spark,
As we trip over boxes, and shout in the dark.
Stuffed toys giggle, wrangling for fun,
In our wild celebration, we all come undone.

So raise up your glass and let joy take flight,
In our jolly chaos, everything feels right.
With hearts all aglow, let laughter ignite,
In this whimsical party, it's pure delight!

Heartbeats in the Snow

Snowflakes dance with glee,
While we lose our way,
You tripped on your toe,
I laughed and yelled, 'Hey!'

Frosty friends nearby,
Their laughter rings bright,
You swiped my hot cocoa,
Now that's a snow fight!

With every sneaky glance,
We shuffle and twirl,
Your hat on my head,
Oh, what a wild swirl!

In the chill of night,
We share silly dreams,
Two hearts beating fast,
In these snow-filled schemes.

The Allure of Hidden Glances

A wink from across the room,
Is that a smile or a sneeze?
Your charm makes me dizzy,
Like a winter breeze.

We play a game of hide,
Peeking 'round the door,
Each time I catch your eye,
I fall a little more.

Lips trying to hold back,
Our laughter fills the air,
Your hand reached for my snack,
But I'm not ready to share!

With every sly remark,
Our secrets intertwine,
Alas, you have my heart,
Next time, I'll take your fries!

Shimmering Threads of Connection

Laughter weaves through the night,
Like tinsel on a tree,
Your grin a shining star,
That's just for me.

We talk of cheesy snacks,
While dodging every glance,
At midnight's silly hour,
We'll lose this merry dance.

Each cookie that we share,
Has secrets wrapped inside,
With crumbs upon our clothes,
We giggle and collide.

A toast with hot cocoa,
To moments sweet and true,
These threads of fun connect us,
Just like the sky's bright blue!

Moments Caught in Time's Embrace

Caught in goofy poses,
We freeze just like the snow,
A thousand silly faces,
That only we will know.

You say I'm on your list,
Of gifts you can't resist,
But you really just want my fries,
Oh, the joy of this twist!

In a whirlwind of cheer,
We caper around like fools,
Who knew such grand adventures,
Could break all the rules?

So here's to all the joy,
Of moments that we've made,
In this funny little dance,
Our bond won't ever fade.

Embracing the Chill Together

Frosty air, we jump and squeal,
With scarves tied tight, we share a meal.
Snowflakes fall, a playful cheer,
Hot cocoa spills; oh dear, oh dear!

Gloves lost under snowman might,
We've twigs for arms; a comical sight.
Laughter rings, it's hard to tell,
If we're playing or ringing bells!

Kisses Wrapped in Silence

A glance that speaks without a sound,
In the winter's quiet, joy is found.
You lean in close, I hold my breath,
But then a sneeze, and it's all a mess!

Chilly cheeks and giggles flow,
Whispers dance where secrets grow.
A pause—then laughter shakes the air,
Your frosty kiss, but are we there?

Echoes of Joyful Laughter

Snowball fights and playful chases,
Tripping over hidden places.
You say "stop!" but I just glide,
With giggling friends right by my side.

We build a fort, it's all a joke,
Until it crumbles, and we choke.
Our laughter echoes through the night,
As snowflakes twirl in sheer delight!

Twilight's Embrace

The sun dips low, our shadows grow,
With silly hats, we steal the show.
You twirl and spin, a dancing fool,
While I just try to keep my cool.

Twilight whispers, we leap and run,
Chasing dreams and winter fun.
But then I trip, and down I go—
A graceful fall, or so it's told!

Sweet Whispers

In the still night, you lean so close,
With jokes that dance like snowflakes' prose.
We play it cool, just you and me,
But then I snort; oh, who could see?

Your laughter sparkles like the stars,
In this sweet moment, we're all ours.
You say my name, I blush and flee,
Yet this sweet chaos is harmony!

Beneath the Twinkling Boughs

In a room where lights dance bright,
Two lovers kiss, what a sight!
But someone sneezes, oh dear me,
A comical twist, how can this be?

With a wink and a nervous grin,
They stumble back, let the fun begin!
As laughter erupts, secrets unfold,
All's fair in love, or so I'm told.

Gifts exchanged with wrapping torn,
Who wrapped this, a total scorn!
The cat leaps on, aids in the mess,
How do we tame this festive stress?

In this chaos, joy ignites,
With silly antics on chilly nights.
Perfect moments, we won't regret,
A memory made, you can bet!

A Radiant Frosted Promise

The frost outside, a crisp delight,
Couples giggle, holding tight.
One trips over a hidden shoe,
Landing in snow, laughter ensues!

A mistletoe hangs far too low,
We all know what happens, oh no!
In crowded rooms, surveys begin,
Who's ignorant and who's got skin?

Nibbles and sips, a feast galore,
But oops! Someone drops a whole store!
A cascade of snacks, oh what a sight,
Everyone's munching with pure delight.

In this frosty winter cheer,
Make sure to keep your heart near.
Amid the chaos and tasty tops,
Who knew love came with funny flops?

Enchanted Evergreen Serenade

In the glow of greens and golds,
A funny thing, a tale unfolds.
Two reach for the same candy cane,
And both end up losing their brain!

With smirks and giggles, they explore,
As ornaments crash from the floor.
A dance ensues, with flair and spin,
One's foot gets caught - oh, where to begin?

The tunes play on, a festive cheer,
Where's the punch? Oh, it's right here!
With every sip, the laughter swells,
This mirth-filled night, oh how it gels!

Under branches, with joy they fill,
Spreading giggles like the chill.
In this woodland frolic, true delight,
May laughter bloom through the night!

Secrets Shared in Soft Light

Nestled close in shadow's play,
Whispers echo in a funny way.
A secret revealed, it swings with grace,
And laughter bursts, lighting the space.

Cheeks go red, a playful glance,
A blind date turns into a dance!
Awkward moments lead to fun,
Two hearts beat like a laughing drum.

Surprises pop like shiny gifts,
And giggles rise, the spirit lifts.
With playful jabs and cheeky grins,
Every joke churns, the joy spins!

Beneath the night, with eyes aglow,
Sharing tales of love and woe.
This soft light's warmth, like a cozy hug,
In a world of laughter, we all snug!

Starlit Paths to Romance

Beneath the twinkling lights we stand,
A chuckle here, a slap on the hand.
You miss your mark with that kiss so sweet,
I sidestep, but now we just might meet.

The snowflakes fall, we're laughing loud,
Wobbling 'neath this festive cloud.
Your mistletoe aim is a comical plight,
I dodge again, but it's all in good light.

With every slip and silly cheer,
We blend our laughs with winter's cheer.
The fans of fortune twist right here,
A cherry on top of holiday beer.

So bring on the jokes, and let bells chime,
A clumsy dance with those out of rhyme.
We twirl and we swirl in this playful jest,
Who knew romance could be such a quest?

A Touch of Magic in the Cold

In chilly air where giggles echo,
You sneeze and spill hot cocoa, oh no!
A finger smudge on your winter nose,
We blush like berries, as laughter grows.

The playful snowballs, a friendly fight,
Your hat flies off; what a silly sight!
We dance through frosty bites and yells,
Antics high on winter's spells.

With every slip, we slide in sync,
Your awkward grin makes me rethink.
A sprinkle of magic in every fall,
A flurry of fun, we'll have a ball!

So grab my hand and take a chance,
In this icy world, let's dance, romance!
We'll warm the air with our hearts aglow,
It's a comedy, dear, this winter show.

The Sparkle of Unexpected Encounters

A chance meeting near the bright storefront,
You trip on your feet, it's a real affront.
With wobbly grace and a comedic flair,
I give you a hand, but you tug my hair!

Amidst the laughter, we stroll down the lane,
You talk too fast, but oh, it's not vain.
With each silly blunder, sparks start to fly,
In this jolly season, who knows why?

The more awkward the tales, the closer we get,
A dance of mishaps, hard to forget.
From winter's chill to warm-hearted fun,
Stories unfold, oh, we've just begun.

So here's to the giggles, the laughter we share,
In this whirlwind of joy, we've found our pair.
With every misplaced kiss, we're finding our way,
Let's laugh through this night, come what may!

Holiday Hues of Passion

Dressed in colors bright, we jostle and grin,
Your sweater's too loud; it's a laugh, not a sin!
With tinsel in your hair, we twirl and sway,
The holiday hues make such a bouquet.

You offer a sip from your spiked cup,
I take a chance, oh, down it goes up!
A hiccup erupts, your eyes go wide,
In this festive mess, our smiles can't hide.

The glow all around wraps us in cheer,
With every wrong foot, I pull you near.
The rhythm of laughter fills this cold night,
In holiday hues, our hearts take flight.

So here's to the clumsy, the cute, and the fun,
With each silly moment, two hearts become one.
Let's dance through the laughter, let's savor the jest,
In this cheerful madness, we'll find our best!

Dreams Weaving through Winter's Veil

In a house adorned with twinkling spark,
Snowflakes dance, leaving quite a mark.
Cookies baking, everyone's a chef,
But the dog just stole the last of the clef.

Laughter fills the frosty air outside,
While fruitcakes sit, with nowhere to hide.
Santas at the mall, they all look confused,
As kids tell tales, a little bemused.

Warm mugs of cocoa, marshmallows afloat,
Yet Aunt Millie insists on her fruitcake boat.
With jests and giggles, we gather round,
In this winter wonderland, joy is abound.

So here's to the snowmen, bright and round,
With scarves and hats all found and unbound.
As dreams weave through this chilly delight,
We toast to laughter, a sweet winter night.

Echoes of Love in Frosty Air

Snowmen frolic, but one looks quite sad,
His carrot nose fell off, oh what a fad!
While lovers giggle beneath stars so bright,
With mistletoe mishaps, oh what a sight!

Cheerful carolers gather at the door,
But singing off-key leaves us wanting more.
Hot chocolate spills as sleds zoom by fast,
And Grandma's knitting? It's a tangled cast!

Jingle bells ringing, what a funny tune,
As the cat takes a leap for the festive moon.
Love is in the air, as snowflakes swirl,
Yet someone slipped—oh, that blonde-haired girl!

So raise your cup for the laughter we share,
With echoes of love and chilly fresh air.
In moments like this, we find our delight,
As winter giggles through the joyful night.

Whispers of Winter's Embrace

Outside the snowflakes gently fall,
While Grandma's fruitcake stands so tall.
Hot soup spills over, laughter fills the night,
Uncle Joe tripped while trying to take flight.

Gloves mismatched, hats perched at odd angles,
Kids in the corner plot tiny wrangles.
The lights blink on trees, a sight so grand,
But the dog's caught the tinsel, isn't it planned?

Presents unwrapped, oh what a surprise!
But where's Aunt Patty? Oh, she's playing spies!
Snowball fights swirl, with giggles and cheers,
As we gather 'round, the warmth staves off fears.

So here's to the whispers, sweet in their grace,
With stories and laughter, we find our place.
In winter's embrace, we cherish the night,
Finding joy in the chaos, a most strange delight.

The Kiss That Crossed the Night

Twinkling stars above and laughter below,
As someone leans in, moving real slow.
A great big miss when the kiss goes astray,
And ends up on the cheek of the cat—what a play!

Mittens tangled, shivers, and scoots,
While snowflakes fall and take root in the boots.
With cheeks so rosy, and hearts full of cheer,
That kiss that missed was still perfectly clear!

Whispers float by with a chuckle or two,
As Aunt May spills cocoa, and friends all go 'ooh!'
The holidays bring such delightful surprise,
With memories made that no one denies.

So, here's to the kisses that took a wrong flight,
And laughter that echoes deep into the night.
For in these moments, we truly unite,
Finding love in blunders beneath the midnight light.

Enchanted Moments Beneath the Boughs

In a crowded hall where laughter flies,
A sprig of green sits, a sneaky surprise.
Caught in a dance, they trip and twirl,
Kissing the air, but missing the girl.

A wink and a grin, they lean in too close,
Only to bump heads, oh what a dose!
Laughter erupts, the room is alive,
While love and clumsiness learn to thrive.

A mistletoe legend, a tale so absurd,
Where teens chase romance, clueless and furred.
Jokes fill the space, with giggles and cheer,
Who knew a plant could bring so much near?

So gather your friends, embrace the delight,
With comedy wrapping you up, oh so tight.
For when you get tangled in laughter and lore,
You might find true love—right out the door!

Love's Illuminated Haven

In a cozy nook where the lights brightly gleam,
Two folks play a game of the old 'candy dream.'
One reaches for sweets, a lofty new score,
But trips on the carpet and lands on the floor.

With twinkling bulbs above, and chocolates in sight,
They share goofy smiles, it feels so just right.
A dash for the fudge, a possible gain,
But instead they just spill it; it's sticky and plain.

The laughter erupts, it's pure silly bliss,
A dodged holiday kiss leads to a miss.
Falling together with marshmallows near,
Who knew that sweet treats could bring such good cheer?

So toast to the moments, the giggling spree,
Where love blooms in chaos and pure jubilee.
Through stumbles and sweets, hearts surely will grow,
While life's comical dance leads to the show!

The Hearth's Soft Caress

In front of the blaze, where the warmth gently glows,
Two friends share secrets and wild little prose.
One wears a hat, a reindeer from head,
While the other just laughs at the silliness bred.

Hot cocoa in hand, each sip a delight,
But whipped cream fights back, what a frothy sight!
It spreads on their noses, a creamy white prize,
As laughter erupts with bright gleaming eyes.

Socks filled with giggles, and stories to share,
With each playful jab, they handle with care.
A casual jest carries them through the night,
As the fire crackles and the stars shine bright.

So cherish those moments, the warmth, and the fun,
For amidst all the laughter, real joy has begun.
With friends by your side and some cocoa to sip,
You'll find bliss in the chaos, let love take a trip!

Glimmers of Tender Affection

Amidst winter sparkle, where snowflakes do twirl,
A couple dashes in, a giggling whirl.
She clings to his arm, he slips on the ice,
With a theatrical fall, oh isn't it nice?

The crowd bursts with laughter, they're tangled and warm,

As snowmen look on, not a hint of alarm.
With mishaps of love that make hearts race,
Every stumble and fumble is part of the chase.

Wishing on snowflakes, they steal a sweet kiss,
While bundled up tightly, they savor this bliss.
In a world filled with chuckles, get cozy in tow,
Where each glimmer of laughter sparks joy in the snow.

So let love be silly, embrace the delight,
With each joyful moment that warms up the night.
For laughter is magic, and love's light will show,
In the cheer of the season, let happiness flow!

A Kiss Beneath the Soft Snowfall

Snowflakes tumble, a dance in tow,
With misty breath, our giggles flow.
Lips meet quickly, a race to start,
Puppies trample, they steal the heart.

A snowman's grin, a cheeky chap,
As we stumble, we take a nap.
Caught in laughter, we trip and slide,
A snowy kiss, our joy we can't hide.

The carolers sing, but we can't hear,
Too busy munching on candy cheer.
In a frosty ballet, we spin and sway,
With each silly kiss, we chase blues away.

Jolly old friends, they toss snow tight,
We duck and weave, what a funny sight.
In a flurry of fun, we love the game,
Sealed with a kiss, who's really to blame?

Revelry Beneath the Winter Sky

Under twinkling lights, we jump and cheer,
With mugs of cocoa, we toast our year.
Silly hats worn, a parade of fun,
As laughter erupts, we all feel young.

Snowball fights yield laughter loud,
We dive and roll, we're feeling proud.
A twirl and a stumble, it's all fair game,
Revelry bright, oh what a claim!

Frosty fingertips, we chase and squeal,
With each flopped kiss, our joy is real.
In a dizzying whirl, with each comical slip,
We ride the joy on a hot chocolate trip.

Underneath stars, we gather near,
With frosty breaths, we dispel all fear.
The winter night, a carnival scene,
Friendship and laughter, sparkling and keen.

Luminous Moments Held in Time

With glittering eyes, the sparkles play,
In a snowflake blizzard, we laugh the day away.
A twirl under lights, such a dazzling sight,
As we giggle and dance, hearts feeling light.

Oh dear, what's this? A slip on the ice,
A tumble, a roll, not very nice!
But laughter will save us, it's magic, you see,
Every fumble a treasure, for you and for me.

With popcorn crowns, we reign supreme,
In our silly kingdom, where snowflakes gleam.
In every snicker, in every cheer,
Moments shine bright, forever held dear.

So let's freeze these moments, just like the freeze,
In our hearts forever, let's savor the tease.
With bright laughter and kisses, our memories climb,
Wrapped in hilarity, held still in time.

The Whispering Echo of Affection

In the silent night, whispers abound,
With playful nudges, affection is found.
A tap on the shoulder, a wink on the side,
In this cheeky chase, our giggles collide.

The echoes of laughter, they dance in the air,
As we tell silly tales, without a care.
A mistletoe prank, who will get caught?
With a cheeky grin, we love this plot.

Snowflakes twirl down, we leap and we bound,
In the frost and the fun, our glee knows no bound.
Muffins and cocoa, a sweetness shared,
In this cozy chaos, we've all truly dared.

With hugs and with giggles, we close the night,
In the whispers of joy, everything feels right.
So here's to our moments, so light and so bright,
Forever we'll chatter beneath the moonlight.

The Promise of Magic at Dusk

As evening falls, the lights blink bright,
The cat's confused by the sudden flight.
Tonight we dance, our moves like clowns,
With jingle bells and silly frowns.

A promise whispered, a wink shared,
A spark of magic, who really dared?
I threw my punch and missed your drink,
Now I'm stuck with a drink that stinks!

With tinsel hair and laughter loud,
We step aside, we grope and crowd.
Oh, what a sight, this dancing crew,
I lost my shoe, but not my view!

A timely toast, we raise them high,
But why's the turkey starting to fly?
Embrace the cheer, don't let it fall,
In this weird ballroom, we're having a ball!

Cherished Moments Beneath the Lights

Amidst the glow, the shadows prance,
We mix our drinks and take a chance.
With every cheer, a clink and spill,
Designed to cause a funny thrill.

The cookies melt, the frosting smears,
I'll laugh instead of showing tears.
An epic fail in every bite,
But laughter wins this festive night!

Your reindeer shirt is far too bright,
I can't quite tell if it's day or night.
We snap our pics, a pose so grand,
Then lose the camera just as planned!

Each moment cherished, every grin,
With goofy hats and extra chin.
The stories shared will last through years,
As we embrace our silly fears!

Frosty Air and Cherry-Berry Hearts

The frosty air is full of cheer,
With cherry-berry bites so near.
Your scarf is tangled, oh what a show,
As we both chase our wayward glow!

A fruity drink that splashed my face,
We laugh so hard, it's hard to brace.
With snowflakes falling, we start to skate,
But why's that penguin parked by fate?

With frosty cheeks, we sing out loud,
Our carols dance, amusing the crowd.
But I fell down, got snow in my hair,
You doubled over, gasping for air!

It's all in fun, the season's delight,
With cookie crumbs stuck in our sight.
Here's to more laughter, mischief galore,
As we stumble and fumble, let's ask for more!

A Soft Giggle in the Frost

A frosty night, with giggles bright,
As snowflakes twirl in pure delight.
With friends around, we paint the scene,
A mishap here, a jolly meme.

Your hat's too big, it covers your eyes,
Yet in this chaos, laughter flies.
We reminisce of times gone by,
With every joke we reach for the sky!

A snowball throws, it missed its mark,
And splattered on the old oak park.
You've turned, with laughter in your throat,
As my mittens freeze, let's play a note!

So here we are, in frost's embrace,
With joyous hearts, we share this space.
Under this sky, a moment caught,
We dance and giggle, a blissful thought!

Heartstrings Tied by the Season

Jingle bells ring, oh what a sight,
I tripped on my scarf, now I'm wrapped up tight.
With laughter and cheer, we dance all around,
Wishing that clumsy folks would never be found.

Hot cocoa spills on my brand-new shoe,
I grin and I sip, 'cause that's what we do.
With pie in my face, I share the delight,
The more that you miss, the better the bite.

A cat on my lap, with tales to unveil,
Dressed up like Santa, it starts to wail.
We chuckle and roll, 'til we're lost in the fun,
Forget all our worries, the season's begun.

So laugh out loud and let spirits soar,
In silliness wrapped, who could ask for more?
With bells on our toes and joy in the air,
This season's a riot, nothing can compare!

Radiance in Each Silent Breath

The lights twinkle bright, like stars in a race,
I slipped on some tinsel, it's stuck to my face.
With giggles we gather, in warmth from the cold,
Sharing eggnog and stories we've often retold.

What's that in my pocket? A cookie or two,
I take a big bite, the crumbs fly askew.
A sprinkle of laughter, a dash of sweet fun,
The best kind of chaos has only begun.

Oh, look at the snow, it's a slippery foe,
I waddle and wobble, but put on a show.
With laughter like bubbles, we tumble and spin,
Each moment we share, where the joy may begin.

In clashing and crashing, we find our delight,
The season's a canvas, so colorful, bright.
With hugs and with laughter, we cherish the cheer,
For moments together, we hold ever dear.

A Serenade of Snowflakes and Heartbeats

A chill in the air, but we're warm from within,
With snowflakes as confetti, let the fun begin!
I toss a snowball, it misses my friend,
And lands in a puddle, where giggles don't end.

With scarves all askew, we stumble with grace,
A dance in the winter, what a silly race!
We slip and we slide, but that's just our style,
A serenade played through laughter and smile.

Hot dogs by the fire, we roast with great flair,
But someone dropped mustard—oh, where did it fare?
With ketchup on cheeks, we laugh till we cry,
For memories made are the reason we try.

So let's raise a cheer to the moments we bring,
With happiness soaring, like birds on the wing.
In a world full of magic, we find our own beat,
In a dance made of snow, where our hearts find their heat.

Gentle Touches Beneath the Stars

Twinkling above, the stars share a wink,
While I try to pour cider, I spill in the sink.
With laughter as bright as the firelight's glow,
We snicker and tease, with faces aglow.

Oh, is it too late to fix that fruitcake?
I lost half the nuts, and oh, what a mistake!
We share tales of past years and moments we've known,
With each gentle chuckle, the seeds of joy sown.

A game of charades turns wild and absurd,
I'm acting a reindeer—nobody's heard!
With faces all red and our sides splitting wide,
In love and in laughter, we take it all in stride.

As midnight draws near, and we share a good cheer,
Each hug and each smile is what we hold dear.
With joy in our hearts, let's dance 'neath the night,
Creating our story, in this festive light!

The Spirit of Giving Under Stars

Jingle bells ring, oh what a sight,
Gifts piled high, all wrapped up tight.
A cat in the tree, what a surprise,
With twinkling lights in its beady eyes.

The cookies are gone, what a heist!
Who knew that the dog could bake like a priest?
A friend dropped by, with a fruitcake so dense,
It could double as a fence for a prince!

Laughter erupts as we play charades,
Trying to guess what the cat just betrayed.
A dance in the living room, silly and bright,
We sure drew attention from the neighbors tonight!

So lift up your cup, let the cheer flow,
Who knew gift wrapping came with a bow?
For joy in this season is not quite a myth,
Just watch out for the tree, and it's accidental gift!

A Hearth Spilling Over with Love

Crackling fire, socks on the floor,
Grandma's recipe? It's a holiday chore!
The gravy's too thick, but spirits are high,
As Uncle Joe steals the last slice of pie.

Sweaters so bright, they'd scare off the moose,
Last year's gift, who thought it could amuse?
A dance-off erupts to some cheesy old tune,
With moves so wild we scare the raccoon!

We gather 'round, with tales to unfold,
Of mishaps and laughter, and memories bold.
The spirits are flowing like cider from taps,
As Dad's snoring loudly and mom just collapse.

So here's to the love that spills over the floor,
With cookies for breakfast and laughter galore.
The warmth of this chaos, a nugget of gold,
Let's toast to the blunders, as the stories are told!

Embraces Wrapped in the Chill

Snowflakes are swirling, it's a frosty delight,
We build a snowman, dressed up just right.
But the carrot's a gobbler, a squirrel in disguise,
Snatching our nose, oh what a surprise!

Sledding down hills, oh what a crash,
Landing in snow like a clumsy old sash.
Laughter erupts from friend and from foe,
As we all tumble down, covered in snow.

Hot cocoa awaits in the warmth of our home,
With marshmallows dancing, like they're in a poem.
Sipping and giggling, we share every tale,
Of our snowy adventures, that never go stale.

So bundle up tight for the chilly embrace,
With laughter so bright, we'll all find our place.
For nothing's more warming than friends all around,
In a season of wonder, where joy can be found!

Timeless Yearnings in Holiday Glow

The lights are a twinkle, the stage is set,
A family gathering, you just can't forget.
We play silly games, with rules gone awry,
And watch Uncle Ed try to fly, oh my!

The tree's decorated, with tinsel galore,
But somehow it fell and rolled on the floor.
We laugh till we cry, as it thuds with a boom,
Now the cat has claimed it, the throne of the room!

Presents all wrapped, but one's gone astray,
Turns out Timmy hid it, that cheeky display.
With giggles and whispers, we open each gift,
Again with the slippers! A perfect little lift.

So here's to the fun that this season brings,
With cherished moments and all of our flings.
For in this pure madness, we'll find that we know,
The joy of togetherness, in the holiday glow!

Kiss of Winter's Embrace

Snowflakes dance as we sip hot brew,
You're in my space, it's not just the view.
A cheeky grin, a playful shove,
Skate on ice or fall in love.

Mittens tangled, laughter spills,
Snowball fights and playful thrills.
A twinkle in your playful eye,
Did you just steal my pumpkin pie?

Chill in the air, but warmth inside,
You missed the catch, but I won't hide.
With winter's charm, let's make a toast,
To silly times we'll love the most.

So let's embrace this frosty strife,
A kiss of winter brings us to life.
We'll dance and sway till the night is done,
In this winter scene, we'll have our fun.

Whispers of Festive Secrets

Beneath the lights, we plot and scheme,
Whispers of sweets become a dream.
Caught you sneaking that last cookie,
But that grin says you're kinda spooky.

The tree is lit, the tinsel's awry,
Is that a reindeer or a cat that flies?
With jingles loud, let's spill the tea,
Santa's watching—oh, just you and me!

With ribbons and bows, we wrap the cheer,
Each gift a prank, come take a peer.
You'll find surprises, oh what a show,
Whispers abound where mischief flows.

Sipping cocoa with hints of rum,
Tis the season for getting dumb.
With laughter that echoes through the halls,
Our festive secrets, how the fun calls!

Laughter in the Frosty Air

Frosty noses and shivering toes,
In the crisp air, our laughter grows.
Chasing snowflakes like stolen kisses,
Falling again, there's no hint of misses.

With rosy cheeks from games we play,
Hot chocolate splashed on a snowy display.
Dashing through snow, a wild delight,
I swear I just saw a snowman take flight!

Let's throw a party in the cold,
Warm our hearts, let the stories unfold.
In the frosty air, we jest and cheer,
May our joyful laughter resound near.

As icicles form, we'll skip and glide,
In winter's charm, we take our stride.
With giggles and joy, our spirits soar,
In this frosty air, who could ask for more?

Yuletide Shadows and Hushed Dreams

As the shadows stretch and silence grows,
A giggle escapes where the warm light glows.
Wink at the cat who's plotting mischief,
The quiet night hides all of our gifts.

With cookies left out and milk on the floor,
We swear we'll be good, though what's in store?
Santa's a pro, he might just miss,
If we sneak a peek at the Christmas bliss.

The shadows whisper, with tales to share,
Silly secrets fly through the chilly air.
With dreams of joy and laughter bright,
We'll dance in shadows till the morning light.

Oh Yuletide laughs, so sweet, so sly,
Let's chase away the sleep and sigh.
In this magical night, let's run and scheme,
In yuletide shadows, we'll live our dream.

Festive Embraces and Dreamy Stares

A twinkle of lights, oh what a sight,
Caught in the chaos, we dance all night.
With cookies in hand, and laughter so loud,
We stumble and giggle, so merry, so proud.

A hat that's too big, it slips down my face,
I trip on my joy, and still keep my pace.
With drinks that are fizzy, we cheer with a clink,
Then spill all our secrets, too tipsy to think.

Hearts play a tune, while the punch bowl awaits,
The pets get involved, causing unruly states.
A dance with a broom, I swirl and I glide,
In this merry mess-up, I take so much pride.

So here's to the moments, ridiculous cheer,
Celebrations of love that only grow near.
Let's toast to the memories we create every year,
With crushes and giggles, and plenty of beer.

A Tapestry of Love in the Snow

Snowflakes are falling, what a wild ride,
My scarf is too long, it wraps like a tide.
With snowballs a-flying, and cheeks all aglow,
We trip in the drifts, putting on a show.

Hot cocoa in hand, I spill on my clothes,
A marshmallow war, everyone knows!
Sneaky little snowmen begin to appear,
I fashioned a cone hat, now laugh—we're all here!

Sledding down hills, we scream like mad fools,
Slipping and sliding, defying the rules.
With noses all pink, we sit 'round the fire,
And swap silly stories that never get dire.

So raise up a cheer to our snowy delight,
With friendship and fun, we shine through the night.
In this jolly adventure, my heart feels so free,
Laughter and love, the sweet recipe.

Mirth and Magic Beneath the Moon

The moon's in a giggle, lighting our way,
With shadows that prance, and laughter at play.
The stars dance around, like they're teasing the night,
As we caper and twirl, oh what a sight!

A snowman named Bob spins tales of delight,
While we spin in circles, our faces are bright.
The crisp air is filled with joy and sweet glee,
As we dance with abandon, just you and me.

With ornaments glowing in whimsical form,
We imitate trees, and we wave in a swarm.
Each twirl brings a chuckle, each giggle a cheer,
In this magical moment, love draws us near.

So let's raise our voices, let merriment swell,
In this holiday madness, all's silly and well.
The mirth and the magic, oh, how they collide,
Beneath the bright moon, with you by my side.

Heartbeats in Harmony with Nature

Out in the wild, where the fun never stops,
A snowman's a show-off with big, silly props.
He flexes his arms made of carrot and stone,
As kids laugh and tumble, no one feels alone.

The trees whisper secrets, they're gossips, it seems,
While we sip on hot cider and chase all our dreams.
A squirrel steals a cookie, oh what a cheek!
While we roll on the ground, play hide-and-seek.

With mittens that mismatch and hats askew,
We carve out some angels, our cheeks rosy hue.
The air is electric, with joy all around,
As we dance in the snow, and our laughter resounds.

So here's to the wild, where nature's our friend,
With flakes on our noses, this joy will not end.
With heartbeats in harmony, let's shout and declare,
That laughter and love are the best winter fare!

An Invitation to Savor the Evening

Come gather 'round, my jolly friends,
With laughter loud, the fun never ends.
We'll sip on punch and wear silly hats,
Dance like penguins, and giggle like brats.

In cozy corners, we'll tell a tale,
Of the time the cat dressed as a whale.
We'll munch on cookies, a sugary spree,
And plot to prank the old Christmas tree.

So bring your quirks, your sass, your cheer,
Let's make this night one to revere!
With mistletoe mischief and joy in sight,
We'll laugh and toast 'til the morning light.

So grab a buddy, don't be shy,
Join in the fun, let out a sigh.
If you've got a joke, now's the time to share,
With giggles abound, it's a party affair!

Shadows of Celebration and Delight

In the corner, a shadow hops,
Gingerbread men doing backflops.
The tree is twinkling, lights gone wild,
That squirrel outside is looking riled.

While we wrap gifts with tape on our chin,
Unruly laughter, let the fun begin!
Someone's sweater is way too tight,
But who cares? We will dance all night.

The pies are doomed, they won't survive,
Silly yet sweet, like bees they thrive.
We'll swap the tales of our crazy dives,
As shadows of delight keep our hope alive.

So grab some friends, it's time to cheer,
With wacky joy, let's spread some cheer!
Each bump and slip, let's not forget,
These funny moments, our sweet vignette.

The Glow of Hope and Togetherness

With sparkles bright, we gather here,
Bonkers laughter, holiday cheer.
It's not just gifts, but silly pranks,
As we toast to joy, with happy flanks.

The glow of hope wraps us in fun,
We play charades 'til we come undone.
The singing's loud, it sounds like cats,
Yet we all join in, even chubby rats.

As cookies crumble and icing flies,
We laugh and roll like silly pies.
In this warm space, we're all aglow,
Creating memories that always flow.

So lift your glass, make a funny face,
In this jolly time, we find our place.
Each chuckle shared, we're wiser too;
In laughter, hope glitters, and friendship's true!

Hushed Wishes Beneath the Pines

Beneath the boughs, we whisper loud,
Hushed wishes stirring, joy unbowed.
With secret giggles, conspiracies blend,
Let's hope for gifts we can all defend.

A clumsy moment, someone trips,
But just like butter, we laugh and slip.
As firelight dances, stories take flight,
Silly wishes, high hopes in sight.

The snacks are aplenty, the punch is strong,
To find the gift, do we play along?
The cat had swiped the big surprise,
Fancy feasts aren't all that arise.

So here we sit, beneath the trees,
With laughter's buzz, we find our ease.
As hushed wishes flit, oh, what a night!
Together at last, our hearts feel light!

Boughs Adorned with Hope

In the corner, the lights are bright,
A fruitcake sits, quite a fright.
Mismatched socks on the floor,
Grandma's snoring, what a roar!

Elves are plotting a grand escape,
With candy canes in a drape.
The turkey's dancing, but alas,
It's burnt so well, it won't pass!

Socks and mittens hung with care,
An awkward uncle's crazy hair.
Gifts are wrapped with tape galore,
What treasures lie behind the door?

Laughter echoes in every room,
Even the cat's caught in the zoom.
With cheer to spread and smiles that grow,
We find joy in this silly show.

A Dance of Hearts in December

The snowflakes twirl in silly spins,
While the dog dreams of holiday wins.
A cousin slips on the icy step,
With a laugh, we won't forget that rep!

Gingerbread men run from the tray,
While kids plot to eat them all day.
Mom is mixing, a flour fight,
Now we've got a snowy sight!

Bells are ringing, but no one hears,
As Uncle Joe spills the holiday beers.
We dance to tunes from long ago,
While the cat looks on, quite in woe.

In the chaos, we find the grace,
Of cozy hugs in this wild place.
With goofy grins and hearts that shine,
December's dance is truly divine!

Wishes Wrapped in Holiday Cheer

Fridge is stocked with pie and cake,
Forget the diet, for goodness' sake!
A tree so tall, it leans to the side,
Hidden gifts there, all snuggled inside.

Jingle bells sound like a cat's chase,
While we all laugh at the dog's face.
A snowman made of our old clothes,
With a carrot nose that always knows!

Tick-tock goes the clock on the wall,
Presents stacked up, they may fall.
Grandpa's snoring, we can't refrain,
From laughing at his silly train.

Let's toast to love, and all things bright,
With goofy games, we share our light.
Dancing in socks, we have no fear,
Wrapping wishes in hearty cheer!

Frosty Dreams and Warm Touches

Outside, the chill ticks off the trees,
While inside we sip on hot teas.
Uncle Bob's jokes, a little hard,
He thinks he's quite the Christmas bard!

In the kitchen, spills and thrills,
A sister's baking, with all the skills.
Cookies shaped like reindeers fly,
Watch out for icing! Oh my, oh my!

Snowball fights break out with glee,
A plump snowman is our decree.
But wait, what's that? Auntie's here too,
Watch her dance, with one shoe askew!

With laughter loud and hearts so bold,
These frosty dreams, they never get old.
In this warmth, our spirits engage,
Together we smile, through every page.

Golden Light in a Silver World

In a world where snowflakes twirl,
Laughter mixes with a whirl.
Chasing pigeons, dodging trees,
Hoping for a sneeze!

Scarves wrapped tight, but noses red,
Tripping over boots instead.
Hot cocoa drips down my chin,
Did I just let the fun begin?

Random snowball fights ignite,
Cheeks all rosy, what a sight.
Feeling joyful, feeling spry,
Who knew snow could make us fly?

At night, the lights begin to twinkle,
As couples giggle, hearts all crinkle.
Swirling in the snowy night,
What a cozy, funny fright!

The Dance of Hope and Memory

With shoes that squeak on frosty floors,
We spin and twirl, and open doors.
Imagining we're oh so sleek,
Who knew we'd hit our peak?

Grandma's cookies, burnt in haste,
She swears she's not lost her taste.
But who can eat those charcoal bites?
A funny sight in winter nights!

We gather 'round the old record player,
Dancing like there's no tomorrow layer.
Step on toes, laugh, and twist,
Each move a charming, silly mist.

With every misstep, every fall,
Those golden memories recall.
In time, we learn the dance of cheer,
Together, silly, year by year!

Frosty Blooms of Affection

In the garden, frost has laid,
Petals shimmer, unafraid.
Roses wrapped in chilly gowns,
Oh, how nature wears her crowns!

We toss snowballs, chase the thaw,
Only to tumble, oh what a flaw!
Laughter echoes through the chill,
It's easy to lose your will!

Watching icicles, pointy and stark,
While we plot sneak attacks in the park.
Wipe away the frosty glaze,
Our hearts bloom in this snowy maze!

When the sun breaks through the gray,
We gather 'round to laugh and play.
In these moments, playful and bright,
Our frosty blooms draw in the light!

Sweet Moments of Glowing Joy

Coffee spills while we all cheer,
With fuzzy socks and chocolate near.
Sipping joy from mismatched mugs,
Stumbling 'round like cuddly bugs!

Giggles float like winter's breeze,
As we swap tales with such ease.
Did the cat just steal my shoe?
Oh, what a funny thing to do!

Fluffy snowflakes gather high,
As we chase the clouds that fly.
Rolling in heaps, a snowy heap,
Waking dreams from our sleep!

Every moment shines so clear,
With laughter that warms, oh so dear.
In these days, we take the time,
To share the joy, to share the rhyme!

A Candlelit Tryst in the Snow

With candles aglow, we giggle and tease,
A snowball fight starts, you fall to your knees.
You aim for my heart, but you hit my hat,
The snow drifts away, where's my cute cat?

Your cheeks turn so red, a bright shade of cheer,
As I throw a soft snowflake, you shout 'Oh dear!'
We laugh as we tumble, all wrapped up so tight,
In the spark of the night, everything feels right.

You trip on a branch, and I can't help but grin,
Say "You're looking like Elsa!" while you start to spin.
A dance in the snow, feet slipping and sliding,
Just two jolly souls, there's no need for hiding.

With cocoa in hand, we dream and we jest,
Who knew snowy nights could be such a fest?
You lean in for warmth and our noses collide,
Outside is so cold, but inside we glide.

Unspoken Words Beneath the Stars

Under twinkling lights, the silence so sweet,
I glance at your face and my heart skips a beat.
You catch me a-gazing, and I turn away fast,
Caught up in the moment, will this feeling last?

The stars seem to wink, as if in on our game,
You chuckle and say, "This isn't quite lame!"
But my heart's in a tizzy, unspoken for sure,
What if I told you? Ah, that's quite a lure.

The air's thick with laughter, but breathless we sit,
"Should I go for a kiss, or just say, 'I quit'?"
You let out a snort, then you blush bright as day,
We'd laugh till we cry, in our silly ballet.

Yet time inches forward, as moments we steal,
With unspoken words, it's the fun that we feel.
I nudge you a bit, "Come on, make your move!"
And you shake your head, but with nothing to prove.

Dreams Kindled by Holiday Glow

Around the fireplace, we tell tales of glee,
Hot marshmallows float, oh, what a sight to see!
You spill cocoa all over your lap, what a mess,
And then laugh so hard, it's a cocoa-drenched dress!

We try to get serious, the moment feels right,
But you sneeze with a giggle, and we burst out in fright.
I chuckle at you, with your powdered-up face,
We're just two goofballs, embracing our space.

Let's toss out the rules, bring jammies to wear,
Forget about glam, we'll parade without care.
You whisper sweet dreams, yet I snore like a beast,
While candy canes dangle, we feast till we're pleased.

With laughter our fuel, we'll conquer the night,
In dreams kindled bright, everything feels right.
As promise of fun dances just out of sight,
Holiday mischief, oh what a delight!

Tinsel Threads of Connection

Tangled in tinsel, a shiny gold mess,
You try to look serious, but giggles confess.
Chasing the doggo, we dance round and round,
With bursts of shrieks, oh the joy that we found.

The tree's standing proud, its lights all aglow,
You get wrapped in garland and then strike a pose.
I'll snap a quick pic, it'll be our next meme,
Holiday fun captured, like ice cream a dream.

We toss shiny ornaments, see who can score,
Best out of three, oh, who could ask for more?
As laughter erupts and the tunes start to play,
We know this connection will never decay.

With tinsel threads binding, we share joyful cheers,
Through quirky adventures and sweet holiday tears.
Let's raise up a toast to our bright shining glow,
In this merry moment, together we flow.

Milton Keynes UK
Ingram Content Group UK Ltd.
UKHW021842151124
451262UK00014B/1269